A DAY in
A ROMAN CENTURION

Richard Wood
Illustrated by Adam Hook

HODDER Wayland
an imprint of Hodder Children's Books

A Day in the Life of

Titles in this series

A Roman Centurion

A Tudor Criminal

A World War II Evacuee

Editor: Jason Hook
Designer: Jan Sterling
Picture Research: Shelley Noronha

First published in Great Britain in 1999 by Wayland Publishers Ltd
First published in paperback in 2000 by Wayland Publishers Ltd
This edition reprinted in 2002 by Hodder Wayland, an imprint of
Hodder Children's Books, 338 Euston Road, London NW1 3BH

British Library Cataloguing in Publication Data
Wood, Richard, 1949–
A day in the life of a Roman centurion
1. Romans – Great Britain – Social life and customs – Juvenile literature
2. Romans – Great Britain – History – Juvenile literature 3. Great Britain
History – Roman period, 55 B.C.–449 A.D. – Juvenile literature 4. Rome –
Army – Military life – Juvenile literature
I. Title
355.1'0937

ISBN 0 7502 2675 7

Printed in Hong Kong

Cover picture: (foreground) the centurion; (background) Hadrian's Wall.

Picture Acknowledgements: The publishers would like to thank the following for permission to publish their pictures: AKG London 28 (top), /Erich Lessing 6 (left), 9 (top), 15 (bottom), 24 (right), /Gilles Mermet 29 (bottom); Bridgeman Art Library, London/New York, /Louvre, Paris 7 (left), /British Museum, London 7 (right), /Rheinisches Landesmuseum, Trier, Germany 13 (top), /Villa Romana del Casale, Piazza Armerina, Sicily, Italy 19 (top), /Louvre, Paris, France 24 (left), /Museo della Civilta Romana, Rome/Giraudon 25 (top); British Museum, London 8 (right), 11 (bottom-right), 22 (bottom); C. M. Dixon 10, 21, 29 (top); © English Heritage Photographic Library 23 (bottom); e. t. archive 4, 5 (top), 6 (right), 11 (top), 13 (bottom), 18 (bottom), 19 (bottom), 26 (top); Gloucester City Museum 28 (bottom); Robert Harding Picture Library *cover*; 5 (bottom), 14, 25 (bottom); Michael Holford 8 (left), 15 (top), 20, 27 (bottom); Hunterian Museum, Scotland 18 (top); Museum of Antiquities, Newcastle upon Tyne 9 (bottom); Museum of London 11 (bottom-left), 27 (top); © Trustees of the National Museums of Scotland 26 (bottom); Wayland 12.

All Hodder Wayland books encourage children to read and help them improve their literacy.

- ✔ The contents page, page numbers, headings and index help locate specific pieces of information.
- ✔ The glossary reinforces alphabetic knowledge and extends vocabulary.
- ✔ The further information section suggests other books dealing with the same subject.
- ✔ Find out more about how this book is specifically relevant to the National Literacy Strategy on page 31.

CONTENTS

Meet Gaius, a Roman centurion of the 20th Legion. Gaius serves on Hadrian's Wall, northern Britain, in AD 150. Although he comes from Spain, he must go where the emperor sends him. He would rather it were not this cold outpost. Gaius is thirty-eight years old and has spent twenty years in the army, but he is now looking forward to retirement, marriage, and buying a farm with his pension. As a centurion,

Gaius has eighty men to command. He is strict but fair, and his men respect and fear him.

The candle-clock that appears through the book is a way of telling the time which was invented over a thousand years ago. It takes an hour for each ring of wax to burn down, as you will see.

7am

THE CENTURION

'*Salve*!' calls the young recruit, as Gaius steps from his doorway. '*Salve*!' he grunts in sleepy reply. A biting wind whistles through the fort. It is still dark, and there are flurries of snow in the air. 'Britain,' grumbles Gaius to himself, 'What a place to serve!'

Britain was one of the most isolated provinces of the Roman Empire. It was rich in grain, wool and metals. When the emperor Claudius set out to conquer the country in AD 43, he gave little thought to the comfort of his troops. Many Roman legionaries were recruited from the warmer countries of southern Europe or North Africa. For them, the biting cold of the British winter was hard to endure.

◀ The centurion. His badge of office was a vine staff, used for thrashing any soldier who displeased him.

▲ Roman soldiers defend the frontier of the empire against foreign tribesmen.

◀ Emperor Hadrian, who ordered the building of a wall to mark Rome's northern frontier while on a visit to Britain in AD 122.

Gaius was doubly unfortunate to be posted to Hadrian's Wall. In southern Britain, it was possible to live a civilized life, with theatres, and shops selling luxury goods from all over the empire. But in the north, the forts were isolated. Beyond the wall were tribes of barbarians and, some believed, the edge of the world itself.

The remains of Hadrian's Wall still stretch across Britain for 120 kilometres (eighty Roman miles), from South Shields to Bowness. It was the largest structure of the Roman world. Regular troops like Gaius were stationed at the larger forts. The rest of the wall was defended by 'auxiliary' troops recruited from the local population.

▼ Hadrian's Wall in winter. It was built of stone or turf, up to 3 metres thick and 4 metres high in places.

8 am COMRADES-IN-ARMS

As the men prepare their breakfast of porridge and biscuit, Gaius checks through the weekly roster. Julius and Clodius are on sentry duty at the south gate, Longus is boot-cleaning, while Marcus is on a week's barrack-scrubbing fatigues for being late on parade. As Gaius reads this, Marcus dashes past with the century's eagle standard.

▲ A group of Roman soldiers in camp, pictured on a pavement mosaic.

The barrack blocks, where the soldiers lived, were long, low buildings covering almost half the area of the fort. The centurion had three or four private rooms at one end of a block. The other soldiers were divided into ten groups of eight, each known as a *contubernium*.

Each group of eight was crammed into a tiny dormitory, with bunk beds and a small kitchen. A weekly duty roster, drawn up by a sergeant, was pinned near the door. It listed the soldiers who had extra duties, such as sentries or firelighters.

◀ A soldier carrying his legion's standard. The eagle was the emblem of the legion. To lose it was a terrible disgrace.

◀ Soldiers were paid according to their rank. These officers belonged to the Praetorian Guard, the emperor's personal bodyguard. They were the highest paid troops in the Roman army.

▼ A soldier's pay. Money was kept in a strongroom in the headquarters of the fort.

The roster also detailed 'fatigues'. These were unpleasant jobs, like gathering fuel or cleaning toilets, given as punishments for minor offences such as having dirty boots or marching out of step.

Soldiers normally joined the army at eighteen, and served for twenty-five years. There was no shortage of volunteers. Although soldiers grumbled about their wages, they were much better paid than manual workers and teachers. The standard-bearer acted as banker. He issued the soldiers pocket money from their wages, but deducted costs for uniforms, food and a 'burial club'.

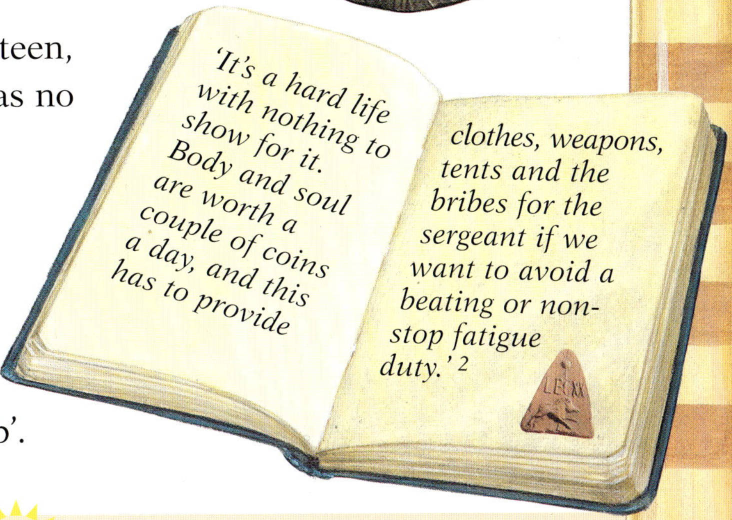

9 am KIT INSPECTION

With their domestic chores over, the eighty men of Gaius's century line up in full uniform outside their barracks. Gaius moves slowly along the line, looking each soldier up and down. His sharp eye can pick out the slightest fault. Suddenly, with a flash of his vine staff, he lashes out at one man's neck. 'Make that helmet shine, Caelius!' he barks, 'And you're on barley and water till it does.'

▲ A typical bronze helmet with a neck-guard.

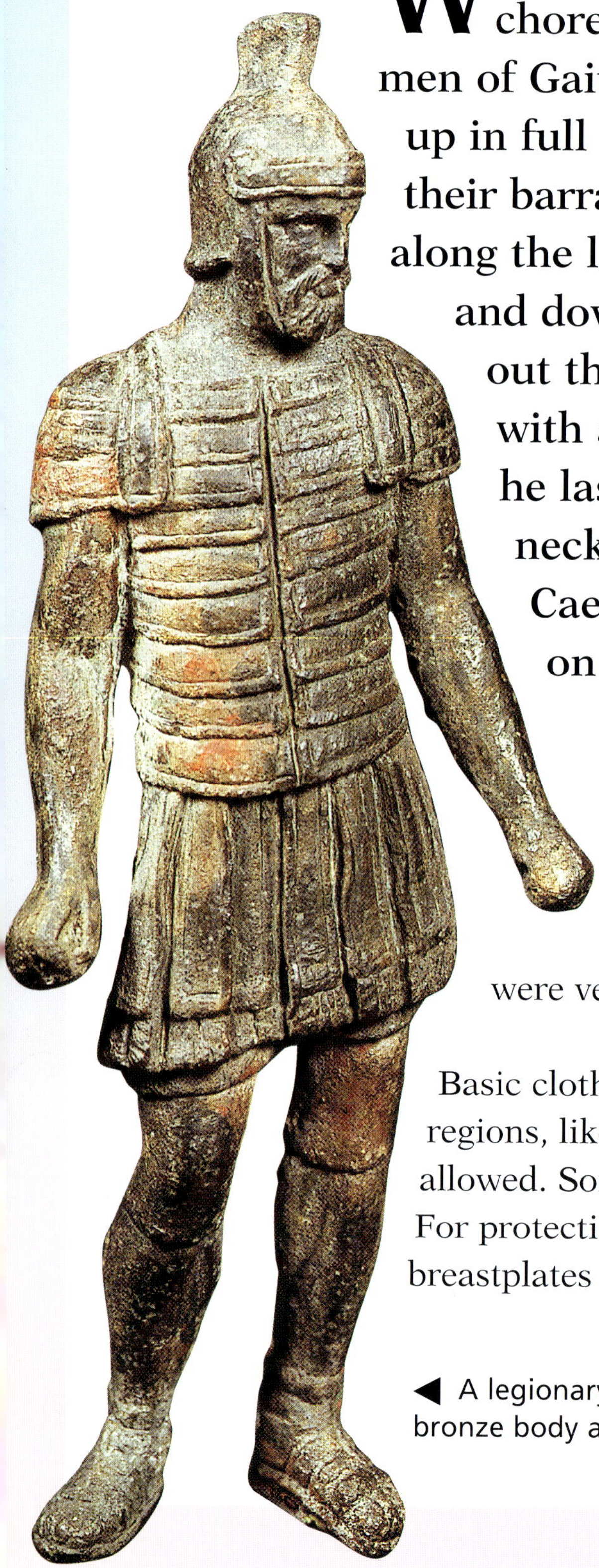

Soldiers had to buy their own uniforms, armour and weapons. It paid to keep these in perfect condition at all times, not only to avoid punishment but because replacements were very expensive.

Basic clothing was a leather tunic with a short skirt. In cold regions, like Britain, woollen leggings and thick cloaks were allowed. Some men also stuffed fur into their boots in winter. For protection, soldiers wore iron or bronze helmets, and breastplates with iron hoops over the shoulders.

◀ A legionary soldier wearing a crested parade helmet and overlapping bronze body armour.

◀ Soldiers in action. The man in front is armed with his shield and *gladius*, or short sword. The man behind carries a javelin, two metres in length.

In battle, soldiers were trained to first throw their javelins. This would break up the enemy ranks. Then the soldiers rushed in close, battering with their shields and stabbing with short swords and daggers. Centurions commanded their troops in battle with strict commands. The punishment for desertion or cowardice on the battlefield was death.

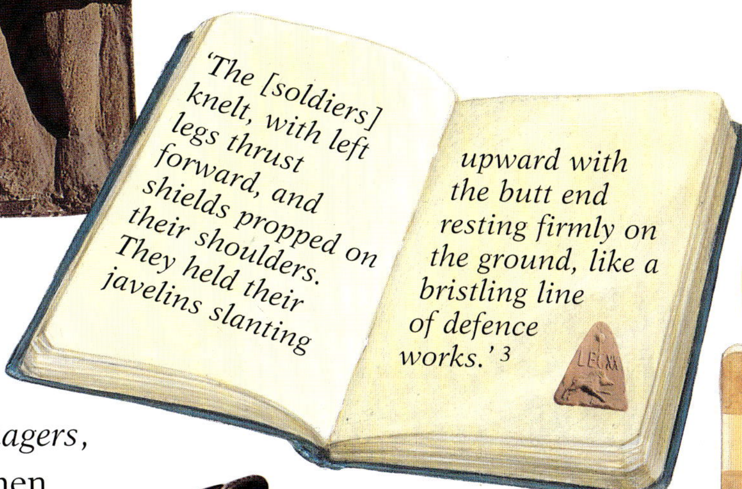

Roman troops were also trained to build and fire huge siege weapons. Catapults could lob enormous rocks over 200 metres. They were called *onagers*, which means 'wild asses', because when they were fired they kicked up like a donkey's back legs. Hadrian's Wall was also defended with *ballistae*, which fired low-flying iron missiles up to 400 metres. These were used to break up charges of barbarian troops.

▶ A model of a catapult like those used on Hadrian's Wall, with missiles and the tools used to load and fire it.

10 am DRILL

A trumpet blast summons the shivering troops to the parade ground. All trained soldiers spend at least two hours every morning on marching practice and drill. Gaius barks out an order to Marcus, the standard-bearer, who then bellows at the troops. They stride past in perfect formation.

On parade, all eighty men of a century had to remain exactly in step with each other. When the column wheeled round to right or left, the soldiers on the outside lengthened their stride and the inner ones shortened theirs, so that no man got out of line.

▼ One drill practised by Roman soldiers was the famous 'tortoise' formation. They held their shields over their heads for protection, and marched in a tight square towards the enemy.

◀ The standard-bearer, wearing a wolfskin cloak. He gave orders to the soldiers while they drilled.

◀ Long, curved trumpets were used on parade and in battle for sending signals and orders to the soldiers. The pig and the ram that you can see were sacrificed to the gods before battle.

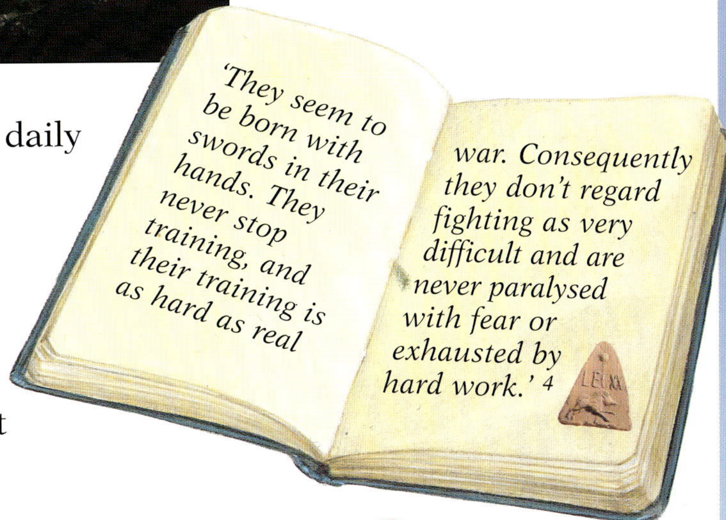

'They seem to be born with swords in their hands. They never stop training, and their training is as hard as real war. Consequently they don't regard fighting as very difficult and are never paralysed with fear or exhausted by hard work.' 4

Rigid discipline, learned through years of daily practice on the parade ground, made the Roman soldier a powerful opponent. Soldiers drilled as they fought, in eight lines of ten men. This tight formation was difficult to attack. It could smash through the ranks of enemies who did not have the same military training.

New recruits drilled from dawn to dusk every day for four months, marching round and round with packs weighing twenty-five kilograms on their backs. They practised their skills by attacking wooden stakes driven into the ground, then fought each other with the tips of their swords covered. It was an exhausting introduction to life in the Roman army.

▲ A tile showing the emblem of the 20th legion.

◀ Soldiers wore sandals like these off-duty, instead of army boots. Constant drilling meant that they could march extraordinary distances.

11am THE COMMANDER'S HOUSE

Gaius reports to the private apartments of the fort commander and his wife Claudia. She is playing with a pet bird and lazily waving a fan. 'My wife wishes to visit the hairdresser in Vindolanda with her slave,' sighs the commander. 'You will arrange a guard for them.'

The commanding officer of the fort had a house known as the *praetorium*. It was by far the most luxurious building in the fort. The praetorium was laid out like a large Roman townhouse, similar to the elegant homes found at Pompeii in southern Italy. Around a central, open courtyard there were suites of offices and private rooms. These had mosaic floors, painted walls and underfloor heating.

◀ The commander's wife. Her wealth is shown by her elaborate hairstyle, elegant clothing and expensive jewellery.

▼ Floors in the praetorium were decorated with beautiful mosaics like this one showing Diana, goddess of hunting.

◀ A Roman lady visits the hairdresser. Keeping up with the latest fashions was difficult in remote places, and women sometimes copied their hairstyles from the figures on coins.

Life could be lonely for the commander's wife. Until AD 197, the commander was the only soldier allowed to get married and live with his family. So his wife and any female slaves she might own were the only women in a camp of a thousand men.

Life was lonely also for the commander's children. They were not allowed to play outside the camp with native children, who did not even speak Latin. Neither sons nor daughters went to school. Instead, they took lessons from private tutors. Children learnt Latin and Greek by writing with a pointed *stilus* on a wax tablet. Lessons were hard, and some girls must have longed for their twelfth birthday – when they could marry.

▶ A carving from the first century, showing children fighting. Roman fathers had complete control over their children, even after they became adults.

12pm

SHOPPING

▲ Shiny red pots called Samian ware were made in Gaul (France) and sold throughout the Roman Empire.

Gaius withdraws fifty denarii from the century's banker, and leaves the fort for the civilian settlement just outside the walls. Seeing the slave of the commander's wife reminds Gaius of Sabina, his own British girlfriend. He had promised to buy her a new red pot for her table, and today is the day when the pottery seller visits.

A permanent civilian settlement, called the *vicus,* grew up round the walls of almost every Roman fort. Here, there were shops, market stalls and taverns. Soldiers could buy luxuries that were not available in the fort, and could socialise with the locals. When they retired from the army, some soldiers married women they had met while visiting the vicus.

◀ Traders, like this pottery seller, took their goods from town to town to sell in the streets.

The pots, pans, cutlery and cooking equipment provided in the barracks were fairly basic. For soldiers with more money to spend, like the highly paid centurions, a visit to the vicus market was an opportunity to buy items of better quality. Traders from southern Britain, or even abroad, made regular visits to sell luxury goods. Local potters tried, not very successfully, to copy the styles of the beautiful imported pots.

▲ Glassware, like this delicate jug and bowl, was imported from Germany or Italy.

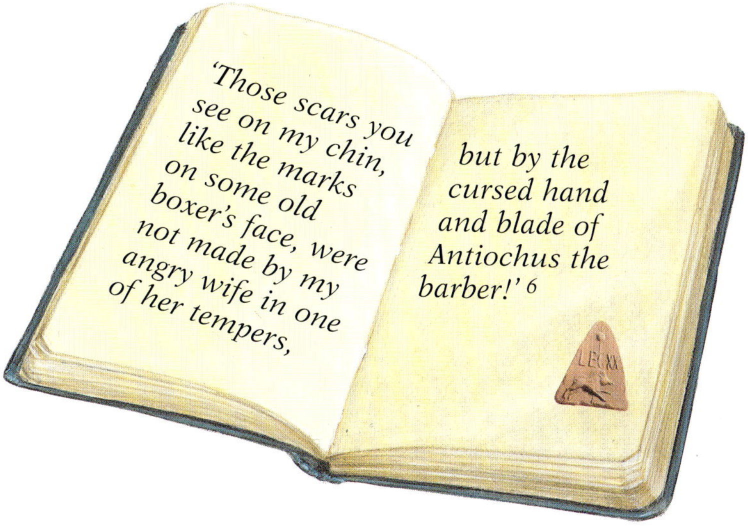

The vicus at Housesteads fort on Hadrian's Wall had many shops, each with only one room. There were bars, a boot and shoe shop, a blacksmith, a barber, and a grocer's shop where soldiers could buy fresh bread, mackerel sauce, olives and wine. It must have been a lively place. Under one shop, archaeologists found the remains of two bodies, stabbed to death and hastily hidden by the murderers.

◀ This carving from the third century shows a Roman grocer selling a variety of fresh fruits and vegetables.

1 *pm* THE VICUS

In the early afternoon, the vicus is at its busiest. Most soldiers are off duty, and like to escape from the camp, for a drink or to meet friends. Gaius catches sight of his standard-bearer, who is supposed to be on fatigues, and strides angrily towards him.

Beneath the walls of the fort, strong smells drift from the food stalls. The cries of shoppers haggling with traders echo around the streets. A patrol marches past and is challenged by the sentries at the gate. Meanwhile, off-duty soldiers mix freely with the locals. Can you find the five characters who appear, along with Gaius, elsewhere in this book? They are described on page 31.

2pm

BUILDING

After a hot snack at the tavern, Gaius heads for the *vallum* defences, south of the fort. A team of builders are chiselling and drilling the stones for the new gateway over the main ditch. 'Take care with the inscription, Favinus,' he calls to the mason. 'I want the record of our work here to last.'

▲ An inscription from Scotland, carved with the names of Hadrian and the 20th legion.

After their morning drill, soldiers often turned their hands to building work. Many of the troops were highly trained surveyors, architects, stonemasons or carpenters. Hadrian's Wall and its vallum (a line of banks and ditches to the south) were built in sections by the Roman centuries. Each century of soldiers built a different section, and they set up inscription stones to record their work. More than a thousand of these stones have survived, telling us the names of regiments and commanders, and the dates when their important work was completed.

◀ Trained to work as a team, soldiers like these could cut stones and build a wall with remarkable speed.

Roman soldiers also built 80,000 km of smooth roads, which criss-crossed the empire from Scotland to the Sahara. They were marked with mileposts at precise intervals. The roads were originally built so that the army could travel rapidly from place to place. But they were also used by the official postal service, the *cursus publicus*, and by the lumbering ox-carts of local traders.

▲ This mosaic from the fourth century shows a team of oxen pulling a heavy load along a Roman road.

▲ A typical minor Roman road, in Sicily.

Roman roads were marked out by surveyors, before gangs of local people or slaves dug out the earth. Soldiers then took over, building up the road surface in layers of gravel and stones of different sizes. The top surface was laid with large stones carefully shaped to fit tightly together.

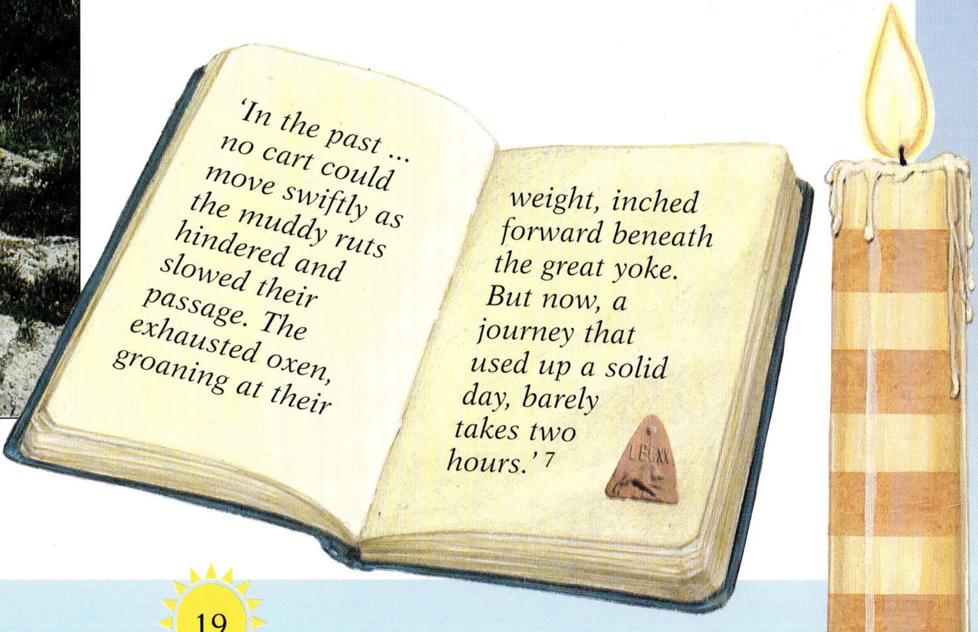

4 *pm*

HOSPITAL

'How, in Minerva's name, did that happen?' demands Gaius. A new recruit lies groaning in the fort's hospital. The plug fell off the tip of his training partner's sword, and his chin is cut to the bone. Ancius the surgeon prescribes poppy juice, to dull the pain while he stitches up the wound.

Evidence from skeletons shows that Roman surgeons carried out quite complicated operations. Their surgical implements, including scalpels, needles, knives, and saws for amputating limbs, were very similar to those used in modern hospitals. But their anaesthetics were poppy juice or alcohol, which only partly deadened the pain. Surgeons were taught to ignore the screams of their patients.

◀ The army doctor was himself a soldier. He holds a scalpel and a set of 'bleeding cups'.

▼ This Roman surgeon's medical kit was found in Italy. The box once contained drugs.

▶ The Romans had many different medical specialists. Here, an eye-doctor examines a woman patient.

Every army fort or camp had its own hospital, called the *valetudinarium*. At Housesteads fort, the spacious, two-storey hospital was built round an open courtyard. Patients could sit here in the fresh air, and it may also have served as a garden for growing medicinal herbs. There were small wards round three sides of the courtyard, a toilet in one corner, and a larger room on the fourth side, probably used as an operating theatre.

Like today, the Romans could buy a wide range of medicines over the counter of their local pharmacy. These were mostly made from plants. One such medicine was *radix britannica*, an ointment made from dock plants and used to treat scurvy. Home remedies recommended by the writer Pliny included gargling with mustard for stomach upsets, and covering the feet with hot turnips for chilblains.

◀ A Roman pharmacist sits in his shop surrounded by the vats and bowls he used for mixing his potions.

5 *pm*

THE BATHS

As the winter sky darkens, Gaius heads out of the south gate to the camp baths. It is hard to keep clean in this muddy landscape. Gaius steps into the steam room, where a soldier is scraping dirt from his body with a strigil.

Bathers had a choice of pools heated to different temperatures, and a hot, dry sweat-room called the *sudatorium*. Often they finished with a refreshing plunge in the cold pool. They did not use soap. Instead, they worked up a sweat, rubbed oil into their skin and then scraped it off. Scrapers called strigils were used to remove the oil, and with it all the dirt from the skin. A centurion might have a slave to perform this task for him.

◀ A bather cleaning himself with oil and a strigil. At his feet is a ball, which he uses for exercise before his bath.

▼ A strigil and oil flask. If people were very dirty, they mixed sand with the oil.

The regimental bathhouse was built outside the fort walls. The huge furnaces that heated it were a serious fire risk, so the baths were built well away from the living quarters or granaries. The furnaces were lit in time for the soldiers to bathe after completing their main duties. There were changing rooms with alcoves where the soldiers could leave their clothes, and a gym where they could prepare for their baths by lifting weights or throwing a ball.

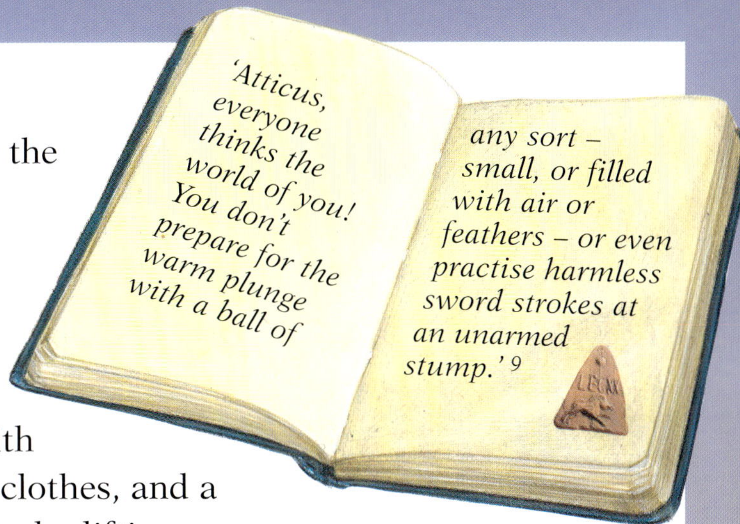

Public toilets were often built near the bathhouse, and were flushed with water from rainwater tanks or waste from the cold baths. Instead of toilet paper, the Romans used sponges on sticks, which they dipped in fresh water running along channels by their feet.

▼ The ruins of the baths at Chesters fort, on Hadrian's Wall.

6 *pm*

MESS MEALS

Refreshed by his bath, Gaius is ready for dinner. This is cooked by the soldiers on 'mess duty', and is served in the barracks. The food is filling but plain: boiled mutton with garlic, washed down with some local beer bought from the brewery in the vicus. The meal gives Gaius a chance to relax with his men, swapping gossip and jokes.

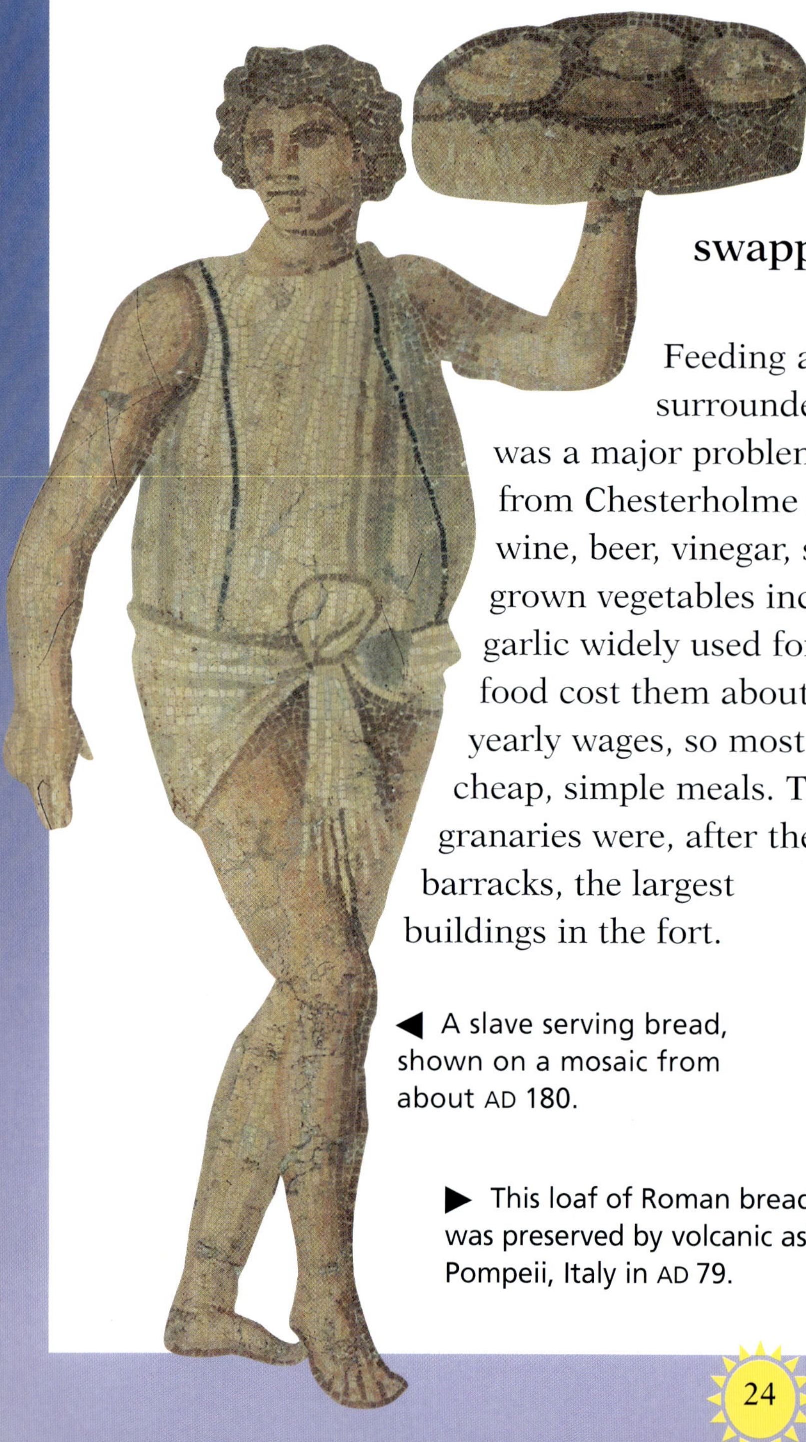

Feeding a thousand men, in a remote camp surrounded by poor farmland and hostile tribes, was a major problem for the fort commander. Accounts from Chesterholme fort record regular supplies of barley, wine, beer, vinegar, salt, fish sauce and pork fat. Locally grown vegetables included beans, cabbage and celery, with garlic widely used for flavouring. The legionary soldiers' food cost them about a third of their yearly wages, so most preferred cheap, simple meals. The granaries were, after the barracks, the largest buildings in the fort.

◀ A slave serving bread, shown on a mosaic from about AD 180.

▶ This loaf of Roman bread was preserved by volcanic ash at Pompeii, Italy in AD 79.

◀ We can still recognize the shapes of the meat joints hanging in a Roman butcher's shop. Notice the scales on the left, which he used to weigh cuts of meat.

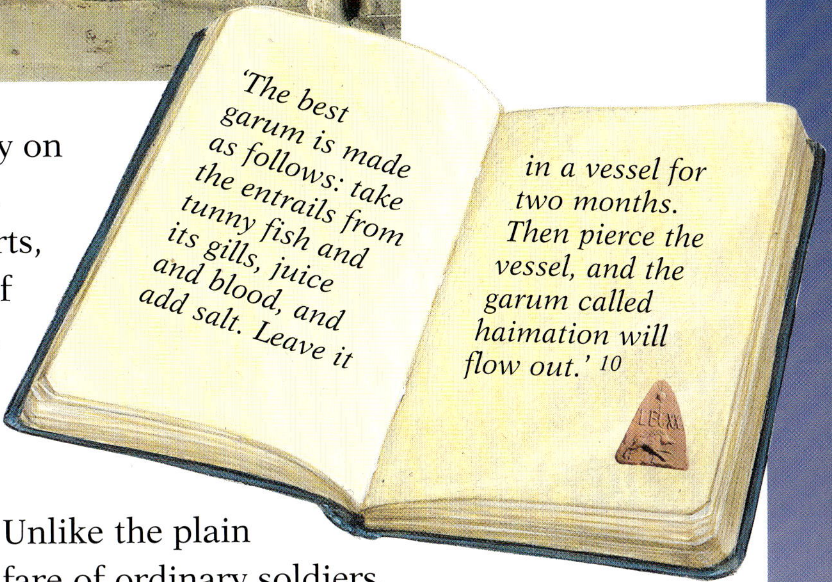

On the march, soldiers were fed mainly on barley gruel and wheat biscuits, which caused much grumbling. But in the forts, butchers prepared generous supplies of meat. Bones found in fort rubbish tips show that soldiers ate large amounts of lamb, pork, beef and goat's meat.

▼ A set of spoons from Roman London. The Romans had no forks, but ate with knives, spoons and fingers.

Unlike the plain fare of ordinary soldiers, the food of rich Romans was quite exotic. Dinner usually had three courses, each washed down with a different wine. Starters might be eggs or shellfish, smothered with spicy sauces. The main course was meat, boiled then lightly roasted. This was also served with strong sauces, containing pepper and the popular *garum* (fish flavouring). To finish, there were pastries, fruits or honeyed cakes. Stomach upsets were common.

8 *pm*

RELIGION

▲ Worshippers lit this oil lamp when asking the gods for their help.

The fort temple is dark and mysterious. Its air is heavy with the scent of burning pine cones and incense. At the far end, a lamp flickers beneath the coloured image of the god Mithras slaying a bull. Gaius lays an offering of food on an altar. The other worshippers remain silent, and the sacred meal begins.

Many temples and altars were built along Hadrian's Wall, where soldiers made offerings to ask the gods for their help. These offerings included gifts of money and jewellery, the lighting of lamps, and even sacrifices of animals. At one temple in Gloucestershire, archaeologists found 150,000 animal bones.

Roman soldiers worshipped many different gods, including Mars, god of war, and Minerva, goddess of wisdom. The Romans even adopted the local gods of the people they had conquered.

◀ Roman soldiers worshipped the gods of the local people. This figure shows Brigantia, goddess of the Celtic Brigantes tribes from northern Britain.

◀ A temple carving of the god Mithras, slaying a wild bull. According to an inscription, this carving was donated to the temple by a soldier from the 2nd Legion.

Many soldiers worshipped Mithras, Persian god of light, who was believed to offer life after death. Only men could worship Mithras, and they did so in secret. Archaeologists have discovered the remains of temples built for Mithras at Housesteads and Carrawburgh forts. Under one floor, they found a tomb where worshippers were buried alive, then 'born again' to join in a sacred meal.

If a soldier had been wronged by someone, he might write a *defixio* or curse on a sheet of lead, roll it up and leave it at the temple. He believed that the gods would carry out this curse against his enemy. Such practices began to die out as Christianity spread among legionaries after AD 300. It was probably Christian soldiers who destroyed the Mithras temples on Hadrian's Wall.

▶ This curse, from Bath, asks the goddess Sula to punish whoever has run off with the writer's girlfriend.

10*pm*

A LETTER HOME

▲ Lamps like this had a wick in the spout and burned olive oil.

Gaius returns to his rooms, and with a *stilus* and wax tablet begins writing a letter home. Suddenly, a loud cheer goes up from the contubernium next door. A dozen soldiers are leaning over a gaming board, lit by the flickering flame of a single oil lamp. One man throws the dice and shouts: 'Ha, Marcus! One more game and I'll win that warm coat off your back.'

At night, a few burning torches lit the main gates and streets, but otherwise the fort was in darkness. Imported olive oil for lamps was so expensive that it was strictly rationed. Locally produced animal fats and fish oil made a cheaper, but stinking, alternative.

Most soldiers probably huddled together in their living quarters, trying to keep warm round iron stoves burning sticks and charcoal. Warm clothing was essential for the cold winter nights. Many men wore the *birrus britannicus*, a long, hooded coat, woven in Britain from very thick wool and sold all over the northern empire.

◀ This tombstone of a Roman merchant called Philus shows him wearing a hooded birrus britannicus coat. Soldiers on night duty were glad of similar coats.

▲ A Roman stilus and wax tablet, used for writing.

A centurion wrote his letters home on a thin square of wood covered with hard beeswax. His 'pen' was a bronze stilus, with a pointed end for writing and a flattened end for rubbing out. We can still read letters found at Vindolanda, near Hadrian's Wall, in which soldiers kept in touch with their distant families.

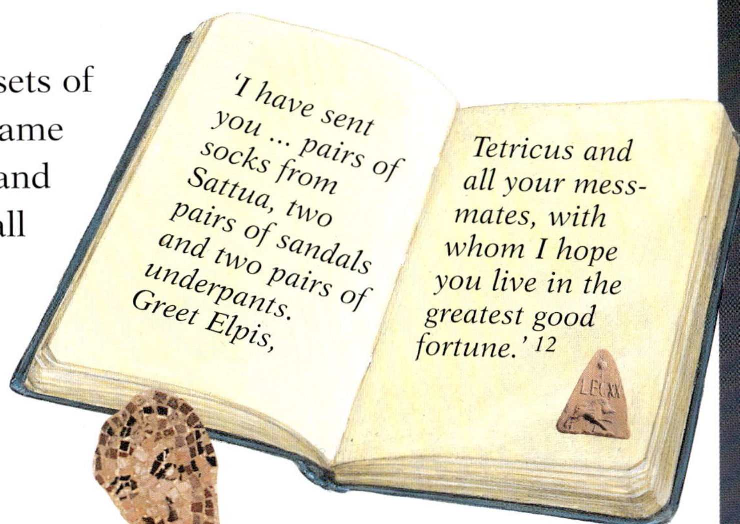

Gambling was against the law, but many sets of dice have been found in Roman forts. A game called 'soldiers' was popular in the army, and some dice were weighted to make them fall a certain way. Most centurions probably turned a blind eye to illegal gambling games, grateful for anything which helped pass the long, cold nights on the edge of the empire.

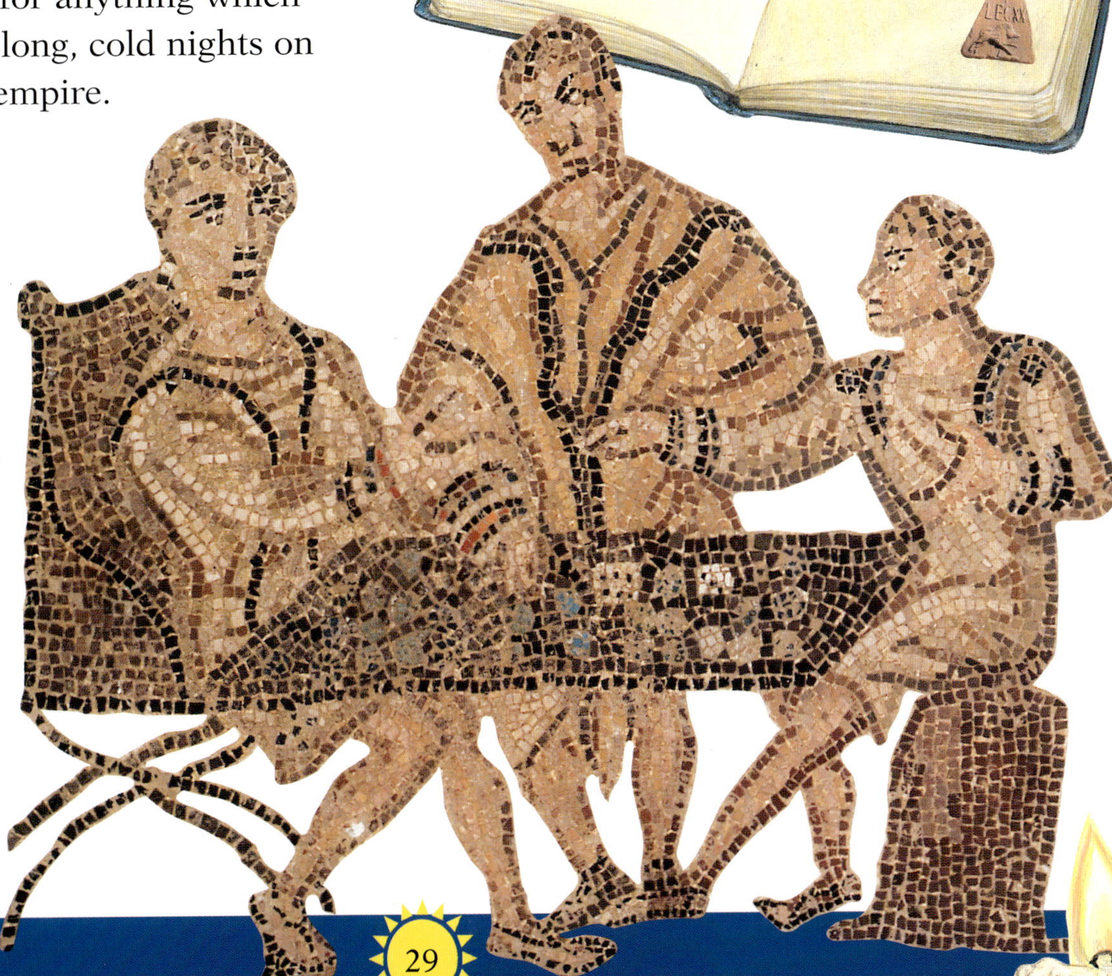

▶ This third-century Roman mosaic shows men gambling with a board, counters and dice.

GLOSSARY

amputating	Cutting off a leg or arm to prevent disease spreading.
anaesthetics	Substances which reduce sensitivity to pain.
auxiliary	Supporting, as in the local troops who helped the Roman army.
barbarians	People of uncivilized, primitive tribes.
bleeding cups	Cups used to draw blood from a patient as part of their cure.
burial club	A club whose members pay in money to pay for their funeral.
centurion	An officer commanding a 'century' of eighty (originally 100) Roman soldiers.
civilian	An ordinary citizen, not a soldier.
denarii	Roman silver coins.
emblem	A sign or badge, like a banner or standard.
granaries	Storehouses for grain (which was used to make bread).
gruel	A sort of porridge made from grain and water.
legionaries	Soldiers of a Roman legion (a division of 3,000–6,000 men).
mileposts	Carved stone posts set along roads to mark distances.
mosaic	A picture created from coloured pieces of stone or glass.
roster	A rota or list of people who had to do certain jobs.
salve	(pronounced sal vay) Latin for hail, meaning hello.
scurvy	A disease, common in Roman times, caused by lack of vitamins.
standard	A distinctive flag, especially of a cavalry regiment.

Many words we use today come from the Latin language spoken by the Romans. Look up the following words in a dictionary and read about where they come from (this should be explained in brackets at the end of each entry): ballistae (p. 9); cursor, public (*cursus publicus*, p. 19); denarius (*denarii*, p. 7); gladiator (*gladius*, p. 9); strigil (p. 22); style (*stilus*, p. 13); sudatory (*sudatorium*, p. 22); vallum (p. 18).

BOOKS TO READ

Hadrian's Wall (A Teacher's Handbook) by I. Watson (English Heritage, 1997)
I Was There – Roman Empire by J. Clare (Riverswift, 1996)
On the Trail of the Romans by R. Wood (Watts, 1999)
So you want to be a Roman Soldier by F. Macdonald (Macdonald Young, 1998)

Children can use this book to improve their literacy skills in the following ways:

- ✓ To compare the fictional opening paragraphs with the non-fiction text, noting differences in style and structure (Year 3, Term 1, non-fiction reading comprehension).
- ✓ To understand that vocabulary changes over time, by looking at Latin words used by the Romans, and how they are used today (Year 4, Term 2, vocabulary extension).
- ✓ To use the footnoted quotes as an example of how authors record their sources (Year 5, Term 2, non-fiction reading comprehension).
- ✓ To explore the use of biography through the role of the historical character Gaius (Year 6, Term 1, non-fiction reading comprehension and writing composition).

TIMELINE

146 BC Roman armies complete the conquest of Greece and North Africa.

89 BC Marius re-organizes the Roman army. Centurions now command 80 men, not 100.

55 BC Roman armies under Julius Caesar invade Britain, but then withdraw.

51 BC Caesar's army completes conquest of Gaul (modern France).

AD 43 Emperor Claudius, with 40,000 men, invades southern Britain.

79 Pompeii, in Italy, is destroyed by the eruption of the volcano Vesuvius.

113 Trajan's Column is erected in Rome, showing scenes of army life.

122 Emperor Hadrian orders the building of Hadrian's Wall.
Legionary soldiers are paid 300 denarii per year, auxiliaries about 100 denarii.

126 The main sections of Hadrian's Wall are complete.

142 Emperor Antoninus orders the building of the Antonine Wall, north of Hadrian's Wall, across southern Scotland.

c. 180 The Antonine Wall is abandoned.

197 The Roman army throughout the empire totals thirty-three legions (180,000 men).
New rules allow soldiers to marry.

337 Christianity becomes the official religion of the Roman Empire.
Vegetius describes army rules and life in his military manual.

410 Emperor Honorius withdraws the last Roman legionary soldiers from Britain.

VICUS CHARACTERS

The characters who appear both elsewhere in the book and on pages 16–17 are (left to right): the standard-bearer, drinking in the tavern, with his standard leaning against the wall (a terrible offence); the potter, arguing with a customer who wants a broken pot replaced; the surgeon, carrying his box of implements, being asked by a soldier to return to the fort; a soldier carrying a pig's-bladder football, heading to the baths followed by a slave carrying his oil and strigil; the commander's wife with her slave at a food stall.

SOURCES OF QUOTES

1. *Life of Agricola* by Publius Cornelius Tacitus (c. AD 55–120).
2. *A Soldier's Complaint*, reported by Tacitus, *Annals* II, 16.
3. *History of Rome* Livy (59 BC–AD 17) VIII, 8.
4. *History of the Jewish War* by Flavius Josephus (c. AD 37–100).
5. From the tomb of a Roman lady.
6. *Epigrams* by the Roman poet Marcus Martial (c. 40–104).
7. *Silvae IV*, iii, by Publius Statius, a poet from Naples (c. 45–96).
8. Quoted in *Roman Britain* by Kenneth Branigan, p. 202 (Reader's Digest Association, 1980).
9. Martial, *Letters* 7. 32.
10. *Of Culinary Matters*, one of the world's first cookery books, written by Roman gourmet Marcus Gavius Apicius (AD 14–37).
11. A lead *defixio* (curse) from Moorgate, London.
12. Letter to a Roman soldier at Vindolanda.

INDEX

Numbers in **bold** refer to pictures and captions.